Francis Frith's
Aylesbury

Photographic Memories

Francis Frith's
Aylesbury

Martin Andrew

FRITH
BOOK Co

First published in the United Kingdom in 2000 by
Frith Book Company Ltd

British Library Cataloguing in Publication Data

Francis Frith's Aylesbury
Martin Andrew
ISBN 1-85937-227-9

Frith Book Company Ltd
Frith's Barn, Teffont,
Salisbury, Wiltshire SP3 5QP
Tel: +44 (0) 1722 716 376
Email: info@frithbook.co.uk
www.frithbook.co.uk

Printed and bound in Great Britain

Front Cover: The Bell Hotel 1921 70563

Contents

Francis Frith: *Victorian Pioneer*

FRANCIS FRITH, Victorian founder of the world-famous photographic archive, was a complex and multi-talented man. A devout Quaker and a highly successful Victorian businessman, he was both philosophic by nature and pioneering in outlook.

By 1855 Francis Frith had already established a wholesale grocery business in Liverpool, and sold it for the astonishing sum of £200,000, which is the equivalent today of over £15,000,000. Now a multi-millionaire, he was able to indulge his passion for travel. As a child he had pored over travel books written by early explorers, and his fancy and imagination had been stirred by family holidays to the sublime mountain regions of Wales and Scotland. 'What a land of spirit-stirring and enriching scenes and places!' he had written. He was to return to these scenes of grandeur in later years to 'recapture the thousands of vivid and tender memories', but with a different purpose. Now in his thirties, and captivated by the new science of photography, Frith set out on a series of pioneering journeys to the Nile regions that occupied him from 1856 until 1860.

Intrigue and Adventure

He took with him on his travels a specially-designed wicker carriage that acted as both dark-room and sleeping chamber. These far-flung journeys were packed with intrigue and adventure. In his life story, written when he was sixty-three, Frith tells of being held captive by bandits, and of fighting 'an awful midnight battle to the very point of surrender with a deadly pack of hungry, wild dogs'. Sporting flowing Arab costume, Frith arrived at Akaba by camel seventy years before Lawrence, where he encountered 'desert princes and rival sheikhs, blazing with jewel-hilted swords'.

During these extraordinary adventures he was assiduously exploring the desert regions bordering the Nile and patiently recording the antiquities and peoples with his camera. He was the first photographer to venture beyond the sixth cataract. Africa was still the mysterious 'Dark Continent', and Stanley and Livingstone's historic meeting was a decade into the future. The conditions for picture taking confound belief. He laboured for hours in his wicker dark-room in the sweltering heat of the desert, while the volatile chemicals fizzed dangerously in their trays. Often he was forced to work in remote tombs and caves where conditions were cooler. Back in London he exhibited his photographs and was 'rapturously cheered' by members of the Royal Society. His reputation as a photographer was made overnight. An eminent modern historian has likened their impact on the population of the time to that on our own generation of the first photographs taken on the surface of the moon.

Venture of a Life-Time

Characteristically, Frith quickly spotted the opportunity to create a new business as a specialist publisher of photographs. He lived in an era of immense and sometimes violent change. For the poor in the early part of Victoria's reign work was a drudge and the hours long, and people had precious little free time to enjoy themselves. Most had no transport other than a cart or gig at their disposal, and had not travelled far beyond the

boundaries of their own town or village. However, by the 1870s, the railways had threaded their way across the country, and Bank Holidays and half-day Saturdays had been made obligatory by Act of Parliament. All of a sudden the ordinary working man and his family were able to enjoy days out and see a little more of the world.

With characteristic business acumen, Francis Frith foresaw that these new tourists would enjoy having souvenirs to commemorate their days out. In 1860 he married Mary Ann Rosling and set out with the intention of photographing every city, town and village in Britain. For the next thirty years he travelled the country by train and by pony and trap, producing fine photographs of seaside resorts and beauty spots that were keenly bought by millions of Victorians. These prints were painstakingly pasted into family albums and pored over during the dark nights of winter, rekindling precious memories of summer excursions.

The Rise of Frith & Co

Frith's studio was soon supplying retail shops all over the country. To meet the demand he gathered about him a small team of photographers, and published the work of independent artist-photographers of the calibre of Roger Fenton and Francis Bedford. In order to gain some understanding of the scale of Frith's business one only has to look at the catalogue issued by Frith & Co in 1886: it runs to some 670 pages, listing not only many thousands of views of the British Isles but also many photographs of most European countries, and China, Japan, the USA and

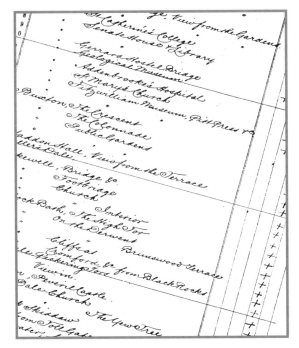

Canada – note the sample page shown above from the hand-written *Frith & Co* ledgers detailing pictures taken. By 1890 Frith had created the greatest specialist photographic publishing company in the world, with over 2,000 outlets – more than the combined number that Boots and W H Smith have today! The picture on the right shows the *Frith & Co* display board at Ingleton in the Yorkshire Dales. Beautifully constructed with mahogany frame and gilt inserts, it could display up to a dozen local scenes.

Postcard Bonanza

The ever-popular holiday postcard we know today took many years to develop. In 1870 the Post Office issued the first plain cards, with a pre-printed stamp on one face. In 1894 they allowed other publishers' cards to be sent through the mail with an attached adhesive halfpenny stamp. Demand grew rapidly, and in 1895 a new size of postcard was permitted called the court card, but there was little room for illustration. In 1899, a year after Frith's death, a new card measuring 5.5 x 3.5 inches became the standard format, but it was not until 1902 that the divided back came into being, with address and message on one face and a full-size illustration on the other. *Frith & Co* were in the vanguard of postcard development, and Frith's sons Eustace and Cyril continued their father's monumental task, expanding the number of views offered to the public and recording more and more places in Britain, as the coasts and countryside were opened up to mass travel.

Francis Frith died in 1898 at his villa in Cannes, his great project still growing. The archive he created continued in business for another seventy years. By 1970 it contained over a third of a million pictures of 7,000 cities, towns and villages. The massive photographic record Frith has left to us stands as a living monument to a special and very remarkable man.

Frith's Archive: *A Unique Legacy*

FRANCIS FRITH'S legacy to us today is of immense significance and value, for the magnificent archive of evocative photographs he created provides a unique record of change in 7,000 cities, towns and villages throughout Britain over a century and more. Frith and his fellow studio photographers revisited locations many times down the years to update their views, compiling for us an enthralling and colourful pageant of British life and character.

We tend to think of Frith's sepia views of Britain as nostalgic, for most of us use them to conjure up memories of places in our own lives with which we have family associations. It often makes us forget that to Francis Frith they were records of daily life as it was actually being lived in the cities, towns and villages of his day. The Victorian age was one of great and often bewildering change for ordinary people, and

though the pictures evoke an impression of slower times, life was as busy and hectic as it is today.

We are fortunate that Frith was a photographer of the people, dedicated to recording the minutiae of everyday life. For it is this sheer wealth of visual data, the painstaking chronicle of changes in dress, transport, street layouts, buildings, housing, engineering and landscape that captivates us so much today. His remarkable images offer us a powerful link with the past and with the lives of our ancestors.

Today's Technology

Computers have now made it possible for Frith's many thousands of images to be accessed almost instantly. In the Frith archive today, each photograph is carefully 'digitised' then stored on a CD Rom. Frith archivists can locate a single photograph amongst thousands within seconds. Views can be catalogued and sorted under a variety of categories of place and content to the immediate benefit of researchers.

Inexpensive reference prints can be created for them at the touch of a mouse button, and a wide range of books and other printed materials assembled and published for a wider, more general readership - in the next twelve months over a hundred Frith local history titles will be published! The day-to-day workings of the archive are very different from how they were in Francis Frith's time: imagine the herculean task of sorting through eleven tons of glass negatives as Frith had to do to locate a particular

See Frith at www. frithbook.co.uk

sequence of pictures! Yet the archive still prides itself on maintaining the same high standards of excellence laid down by Francis Frith, including the painstaking cataloguing and indexing of every view.

It is curious to reflect on how the internet now allows researchers in America and elsewhere greater instant access to the archive than Frith himself ever enjoyed. Many thousands of individual views can be called up on screen within seconds on one of the Frith internet sites, enabling people living continents away to revisit the streets of their ancestral home town, or view places in Britain where they have enjoyed holidays. Many overseas researchers welcome the chance to view special theme selections, such as transport, sports, costume and ancient monuments.

We are certain that Francis Frith would have heartily approved of these modern developments in imaging techniques, for he himself was always working at the very limits of Victorian photographic technology.

The Value of the Archive Today

Because of the benefits brought by the computer, Frith's images are increasingly studied by social historians, by researchers into genealogy and ancestory, by architects, town planners, and by teachers and schoolchildren involved in local history projects.

In addition, the archive offers every one of us an opportunity to examine the places where we and our families have lived and worked down the years. Highly successful in Frith's own era, the archive is now, a century and more on, entering a new phase of popularity.

The Past in Tune with the Future

Historians consider the Francis Frith Collection to be of prime national importance. It is the only archive of its kind remaining in private ownership and has been valued at a million pounds. However, this figure is now rapidly increasing as digital technology enables more and more people around the world to enjoy its benefits.

Francis Frith's archive is now housed in an historic timber barn in the beautiful village of Teffont in Wiltshire. Its founder would not recognize the archive office as it is today. In place of the many thousands of dusty boxes containing glass plate negatives and an all-pervading odour of photographic chemicals, there are now ranks of computer screens. He would be amazed to watch his images travelling round the world at unimaginable speeds through network and internet lines.

The archive's future is both bright and exciting. Francis Frith, with his unshakeable belief in making photographs available to the greatest number of people, would undoubtedly approve of what is being done today with his lifetime's work. His photographs, depicting our shared past, are now bringing pleasure and enlightenment to millions around the world a century and more after his death.

Aylesbury - *An Introduction*

UNTIL THE LATER 19th century, Aylesbury's character as a hilltop town was much more evident than now, when expansion in all directions has blurred its original location. Surrounded by streams and unhealthy marshy flatlands, it was a compact but ancient town in 1837, with a population of about 6,000. When I moved to Buckinghamshire to work for the County Council's historic buildings section in 1978, Aylesbury was at the end of its massive expansion phase; this had started before World War II, but had climaxed in the 1960s. That decade, so fateful to the historic fabric of so many of England's smaller (and larger) historic towns, saw numerous 1960s housing estates, including Bedgrove Park, constructed; also, and more significantly for this book, there was extensive redevelopment in the town centre. This cleared much of the south-west area of the

Market Square and Walton Street.

Unfortunately, this obsession with reviving through wholesale redevelopment rather than through restoration led to much replacement of individual buildings elsewhere in the streets. That said, some areas escaped lightly - this was quite deliberate. The present Friars Square, the bus station and the County Council tower block were the only areas where complete rebuilding was sanctioned on any scale. Hale Leys, built behind the frontage buildings, and the streets north-west of Market Square in particular, retain the character of an 18th-century market town virtually intact. St Mary's Square, Temple Square and the surrounding streets are superb, and the contrast with the crass devastation of High Wycombe further south in the county is very marked.

The 1960s inner ring road in the main

widened existing streets such as Exchange Street, and took many years to complete. The outer ring road provided a focus for housing development, and industrial and commercial estates were grouped south of the Bicester Road and along Stocklake to the east of the town centre. Development and expansion have continued since. The current major area of expansion is the Fairford Leys 'village' west of the town between it and Hartwell, where a highly flawed attempt is under way to finesse a giant housing estate as a purpose-built village; while Watermead, north of the town, was a 1980s version of the same thing. Much more expansion is currently being considered to the north-west.

Like many other towns, Aylesbury expanded with homes fit for heroes after the First World War; the Southcourt Council Estate was laid out in the 1920s by one of the designers of the more up-market Hampstead Garden Suburb. This expanded greatly, and together with other

expansion of private and council housing in the 1930s was followed after the Second World War by housing built for London overspill. The keen student of the old town as it existed before 1900 must peel all this away: we must imagine fields coming close to the foot of Aylesbury's hill on all sides, with only the now subsumed village of Walton anywhere near physically joined to the town.

But let us go back to the beginning of Aylesbury's history. It is situated on a Portland limestone hill, an outlier from the Brill-Winchendon Hills, and a naturally defensive position. It is no surprise that Iron Age settlement evidence turned up in 1970s and 1980s excavations, which led archaeologists to speculate on the possibility of the hill being an Iron Age hillfort; 'bury' in an Anglo-Saxon place name usually indicates prehistoric earthworks. Roman finds are more sparse, and do not yet suggest a Roman settlement of the hill, despite

Market Place 1901 47462

the fact that the road known to the Anglo-Saxons as Akeman Street - which ran from Verulamium (St Albans) to Corinium (Cirencester) via Alchester - passed along the northern slopes of Aylesbury's hill. Fleet Marston, three miles to the west, appears to have been a small Roman settlement at the junction with another Roman road to Lactodurum (Towcester).

However, it is with the Anglo-Saxon period that Aylesbury appears for the first time in written history. The Anglo-Saxon Chronicle records under 571 AD that 'Cuthla fought against the Britons at Biedcanford and captured four villages, Limbury, Aylesbury, Benson and Eynsham'. So Aylesbury must have been a hilltop village well before this, since 'Aegel' is an Anglo-Saxon name. By around 1000 AD, the village had presumably grown into a town, for by then it had a mint; silver pennies produced by eight moneyers have been found. The large church has long been thought to be the

successor of a minster church, which was an Anglo-Saxon mother church serving a large area with little or no parish organisation. These churches are often cruciform, that is with a crossing tower and transepts; other examples include Uffington in Berkshire and Stow in Lincolnshire. This theory received support of a sort in excavations within the nave of St Mary's Church in 1978, which uncovered clear evidence of a late Anglo-Saxon church. One other fragment of non-archaeological evidence is a will of about 970 AD in which Aelfheah, Ealdorman of Hampshire, bequeathed Aylesbury to King Edgar. Anglo-Saxon finds in excavations are slowly filling in the picture: burials have been found within the old town and in Walton off the hill. The town is on a naturally defensive site; did the Anglo-Saxon settlers take advantage of Iron Age ramparts, or did they build their own? Were there any Iron Age ramparts? These questions await answers, I fear, at this stage; but

Church Street c1955 A84036

the very compactness of the town, with the churchyard and Kingsbury market place in the north-west and the later medieval Market Square to the south-east, indicates a firm boundary of some sort, so the theory of an Anglo-Saxon burh is given some credence.

It is disappointing that Domesday Book in 1087 gives no hint of burgesses or merchants; however, it does refer to market tolls with an annual face value of £10. The Middle Ages saw Aylesbury grow into a prosperous market town with two large market places, both subject to encroachment early on. There are timber-framed buildings in the island between Kingsbury and Buckingham Street, and the Dark Lantern has early 17th-century timber-framing from encroachment onto Market Square. Clearly, the town was the market centre for a large hinterland, with its livestock and crops supplying the ever-hungry mouths of London. However, it is a strangely undocumented town. It presumably attained borough status after Domesday Book's time. There was apparently a royal castle somewhere, but its only trace is in the name Castle Street.

There are hints confirming urban life for from 1218 onwards. The Royal assizes were often held in Aylesbury, and the court of the King's bench was held here after 1351. This was part of the gradual supplanting of Buckingham as the administrative capital of Buckinghamshire, and by the 17th century the circuit judges only heard cases in Aylesbury. A Franciscan friary was established in 1286, and two hospitals were established within the town, St Leonard's and St John's. Ceely House, now part of the County Museum in Church Street, was built in 1473 as the Brotherhood House of the Fraternity of the Virgin Mary; the King's Head

was built as an inn in the 15th century, with stained glass datable to 1456. However, the town did not get a charter until 1553, and lost it later through administrative incompetence. The bones of the town were laid; little change in the original street plan took place until the arrival of Friars Square in the 1960s. In fact, there are quite a few pre-1600 buildings apart from the 13th-century parish church: they include a 15th-century cruck house in Castle Street, the Lobster Pot and the Hobgoblin (ex-Red Lion) in Kingsbury, and No 2 Church Street, which is datable to around 1546. We have already mentioned early encroachment on the market places.

During the English Civil War, Aylesbury was stoutly pro-Parliamentarian (there is now a statue of John Hampden, one of the Parliamentary leaders, in the Market Square). It was subject to several attacks from King Charles' headquarters in Oxford, some led by the dashing cavalry leader Prince Rupert. There was a battle at Holman's Bridge, a bridge over the young River Thame on the Buckingham road a mile north of the town, and there are Civil War siege earthworks at Quarrendon.

During the 17th century, there was much rebuilding in stout timber-framing on urban plots. Many of these buildings survive, often now concealed behind later brick frontages; the best of them are, again, No 2 Church Street, with its front of 1739, and Ceely House. By 1800, the town was prosperous from agriculture in the improved rich soils of the Vale; success in corn growing and duck rearing (and also lace making) gave it a wealthy Georgian appearance, a character it has not lost to this day in some areas. In 1718 a grammar school was founded in Church Street, and in 1722 work began on an imposing County Hall in the Market Square as the town assumed the trappings of civic dignity. The County Assizes and Quarter Sessions were held here until they were abolished in 1970; then it became the County Court. It had a first-floor balcony which served as the 'drop' for a scaffold for public hangings. The last public execution took place in 1845, when the 'Quaker' poisoner John Tawell was hanged, having been apprehended in London from a description telegraphed from Slough station to Paddington: an early and sensational use of the new medium.

This smallish agricultural market town, long the administrative capital of Buckinghamshire, was now poised for new growth. The Enclosure Acts had placed farming on a new non-subsistence footing, which resulted in greatly increased crop yields and improved pasture. For example, Acts of Parliament for Enclosure were passed for Hartwell and Stone in 1776, Bierton and Hulcott in 1779, Stoke Mandeville in 1797, Weston Turville in 1798 and Walton in 1799. The canal, first authorised in 1794, opened in 1815 as the Aylesbury arm of the Grand Junction Canal, thus linking the town's trade by water with the rest of the country. The railway arrived in 1839 as a branch line from the London and North Western Railway; its station was originally near the junction of Station and Railway Streets, and was then rebuilt in 1889 fronting onto the High Street near the Exchange Street junction. This line was lifted and the station demolished in 1960; Aylesbury's second station is now the town's only one. This opened as a branch from the Great Western Railway's Princes Risborough station in 1863, which was extended to Verney Junction in 1868. This station also served the Metropolitan Railway, which reached Aylesbury

in 1892 - they rebuilt the station at the same time. The Metropolitan abandoned Aylesbury, only serving Buckinghamshire as far out as Amersham, and the line was taken over by the Great Central for its route to Nottingham and Sheffield. Nowadays, Aylesbury is the terminus of the Chiltern Railway from Marylebone, and only freight goes beyond the town.

During the 19th century the town acquired many public buildings and facilities. These included a new Market Hall in 1806 (demolished in 1866), a gas works in 1834 to provide light for the town, a workhouse in 1844, a modern prison in 1845 (now the Tindal Hospital), a cemetery in 1856, the Royal Bucks Hospital in 1859 and a Corn Exchange next to County Hall in 1865. The quirky architect E B Lamb built Judge's Lodgings in the 1850s. Industry arrived in the later 19th century to supplement cottage industries like Aylesbury duck rearing and lace making. Taking advantage of both the canal and the cattle pastures of the Vale, the Anglo-Swiss Condensed Milk Company built its factory in 1870, which is now part of Nestle's, and Hazell, Watson and Viney built their new greatly-expanded factory nearby in 1878. The High Street had been laid out in 1826; it was originally called New Road. Mainly after 1870, speculators drained the marshy ground and built housing estates beyond the old town centre for the first time. These included Manor Park from 1882 on, Albion Street off the High Street in the 1880s, and Queens Park on the other side of the canal after 1900, while the housing of Victoria Park was laid out on the north side of the Tring Road in the 1890s. These served the new factories at various social levels, but the real growth came after the First World War, and is touched on at the beginning of this Introduction.

From miles around the most noticeable building in the town is the County Council's tower block, a curious combination of old and new: it has bay windows with sliding sash windows, and is surmounted by pitched roofs. It was designed by Fred Pooley, the County Architect, but the job architect was Malcolm Dean, an architect committed to Georgian architecture. Although much hated, it is an interesting building, and the first office block to escape the then-ubiquitous style of flat elevations with coloured panels below their windows. For its time, 1963-1966, it was a humane building; I worked in its upper floors for ten years, and it certainly gave me fine views over the town, the Vale of Aylesbury and beyond. It showed me the jumble of old tile roofs interspersed with slate ones that reassured me that the Georgian town was more or less intact still, despite all the changes that the 20th century wrought in its fabric. One day, who knows, the County tower, Fred's Folly, may be a listed building.

Down at street level we can wander the streets and lanes of the hilltop town and be grateful that so much survives. The two market squares, the churchyard and St Mary's Square are linked by historic streets, for the Friars Square shopping centre only destroyed the south-west corner of the town. Traffic has largely been removed from Market Square, and the upper part of the High Street and one-way systems and loops have effectively reduced traffic in much of the historic core, to its immense benefit. Now it is a pleasant environment for walking around in, so that we can appreciate its atmosphere and buildings all the better. The ring road did damage, undoubtedly, but the core is sufficiently large to be a most worthwhile one to visit and linger in. I enjoyed my ten years helping to safeguard the historic buildings in the town and the surrounding villages; it is my county town, as I still live in nearby Haddenham. It is a thriving and vigorous town, and I hope these photographs convey its rich building heritage.

The Vale c1955 A84047

Aylesbury:
Market Square & Kingsbury Square

Above: **Aylesbury Ducks c1955** A84044
The name of Aylesbury is known to everyone through
its distinctive heavy breed of duck, which was
developed in the 18th century for the London meat
market. They were driven on foot (later in railway
wagons) to Smithfield and other markets. They were
bred in Aylesbury and the surrounding villages,
including Walton and Haddenham, whose ponds were
of great use, and at Weston Turville, which alone sent
25,000 ducklings a year to London in the 1890s. The
true Aylesbury duck is virtually extinct - the last known
flock was at Chesham in the 1980s.

Left: **County Hall 1897** 39626
We start our tour of Aylesbury in the Market Square in
the heart of the town. The south side of the square is
dominated by the Georgian County Hall, which was
designed by Thomas Harris. Work started in 1722, but
it was not completed until 1737: local government has
always been strapped for cash. There used to be a
balcony across the centre at first floor level from which
public hangings took place until 1845.

Market Square 1901 47462x
This is an interesting photograph, for the view has been unashamedly doctored by Frith for the Christmas postcard market to look like a seasonally snowy scene. This was not an uncommon practice, but in this case must have convinced no-one, for nobody is in winter clothes. The 'snow' clings to the Clocktower, whose foundation stone was laid in July 1876.

Market Square 1901 47463

In this view, looking downhill towards County Hall, there is a sheep market under way. Livestock was sold here until 1927; after that time the stock market moved to a site off Exchange Street, now built over by a multi-screen cinema complex. Until 1866 there was a Market House and other buildings in the foreground, which were all swept away to re-open this part of the market place.

Market Square 1901 47461

Beyond the Clocktower, the Georgian brick front belongs to the George Inn, which was replaced by Burtons in 1936. The Freeman Hardy and Willis building still survives, but there has been wholesale destruction of the rest to its left for the Friars Square shopping centre. A cart stands with hurdles for the sheep pens beside one of the French cast-iron lions given by Ferdinand Rothschild in 1887. They were hauled here by steam wagons from Waddesdon Manor.

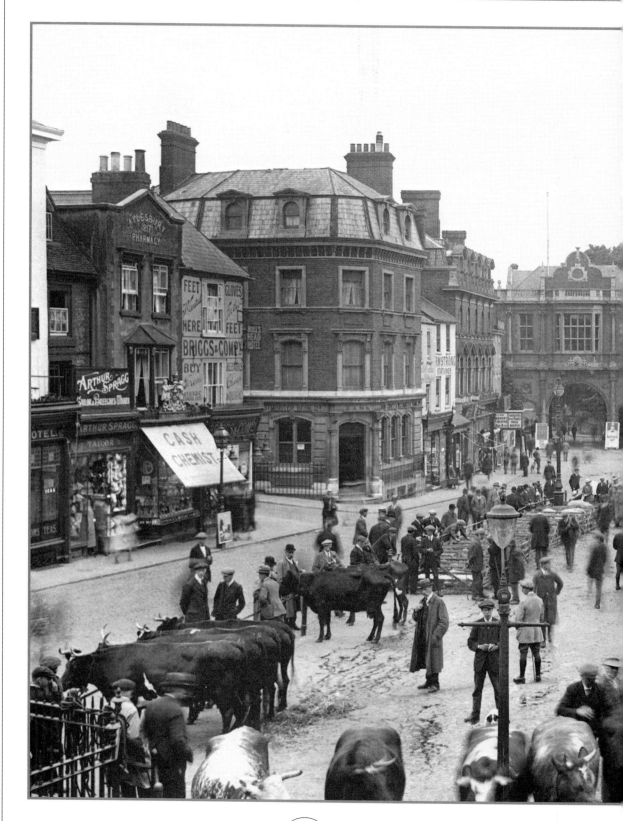

Market Square 1921

70552

We are looking from the north end of the market place. A cattle and sheep market is in full swing. To the left of the Clocktower and the County Hall is the Jacobean-style Town Hall and Corn Exchange building by Brandon, dated 1865. Much of this was destroyed in a fire in 1962, but fortunately the triple archway survives, which supported the upper hall with its mullioned and transomed windows and shaped gable above.

► **The Market Place c1950** A84017
This view is taken from beneath the Corn Exchange archways, which once led to the relocated cattle market some two hundred yards behind the photographer. In 1950 the old market place had become a car park. It is now restored and car free; the central areas are surfaced with Denner Hill setts, a hard stone from the Chilterns above High Wycombe which is used all over the south of the county for kerbs and setts.

► **The War Memorial c1955**
A84026
After World War I, a dignified war memorial was built at the north end of the Market Square with the names of the dead on bronze plaques. It is unchanged, apart from plaques added for the dead of the Second World War. The statue is of John Hampden, the 'Patriot', who was one of the Parliamentary leaders in the Civil War against Charles I. The bronze statue by Fehr was erected in 1911; it was moved fifty feet in 1988 when the Market Place was restored.

▲ **Market Square 1921**
70553
On the right the Market Theatre, now long gone, was behind the pub dispensing Weller's Ales, the Market Tavern. The grand Victorian building to its left, the International Stores, now the Halifax, survives, but all to its left has gone. The scaffolding beyond the lamppost hides Lloyds Bank, which was being extended and restored at the time (there are rainwater heads dated 1921). This bank was founded in 1795; it became the Bucks and Oxon Union Bank in 1853.

◄ The Bell Hotel 1921

70563

To the right of County Hall is the Bell Hotel, a Regency building which was recast in 1919 with the addition of a dormered roof storey. The corner entrance has since been replaced by a window, and a large bell now hangs above the main doorway. County Hall, with the huge urns above the pediment, was gutted by fire in 1970, but its county court interior was restored in every detail - even down to the chamber pot for the judge.

◀ Market Square c1955
A84050

This view looks east past the much-reduced George pub, with Burton's facade beyond, to the junction of Cambridge Street at the left and High Street to the right of the Round House. The John Hampden statue behind the War Memorial has now moved nearer to the Disraeli statue; this is also by Fehr, and was erected in 1914. To its right is the Midland Bank, a Baroque pink sandstone-faced building of 1921.

◄ Market Square c1955 A84005

The white fronted Burton's at the far end is in the up-to-the-minute Art Deco style favoured by the tailoring company all over the country. Its foundation stone was laid in 1936 by Stanley Howard Burton himself. The Industrial Photographers on the left have taken over from Freeman Hardy and Willis's shoeshop. Since the time of this view, the building has been stripped of all adornment and rendered, but the Victorian building on the right behind Boots survives in all its Italianate splendour above shop level.

► Market Square c1955

A84032

Between the lions is a statue of Major-General Charles Compton, third Baron Chesham, the commander of the Bucks Militia, who fought in South Africa during the Boer War. This good bronze by Tweed was unveiled in 1910; it still surveys the square, although the low stone walls either side of the plinth have been removed.

◄ Market Square c1965

A84084

Ten years after photograph No A84005, the Market Square is even more choked by cars. Beyond the scooter and bubble car which so strongly evoke the 1960s, the theatre has become the Embassy Grill. Pettit's Stores on the right is now the Grapes and a barber's shop. This view captures the Market Square just before the wholesale redevelopment of Aylesbury got under way, destroying many of the buildings fronting the market place.

▶ **The King's Head Hotel, the Ancient Window 1901**
47466
The King's Head is one of Aylesbury's architectural treasures; it is tucked away off the Market Square. This view shows the 15th-century great hall window, ten lights wide with arched upper lights. Some original glass survives, including armorial glass with the coat of arms of Henry VI and Margaret of Anjou, which dates from 1456: a remarkable and rare survival amid the bustle of an inn through over five and a half centuries.

▶ **Ye Olde King's Head Hotel c1955** A84030
After years as a pub and hotel, the King's Head underwent major and scholarly restoration in the 1990s, and the front is now coated overall with yellow ochre limewash. Here the photographer looks down the alley from Market Square to the entrance bay; the oriel window was added by George Devey for the Rothschilds in the 1870s. The building on the left was demolished in 1962.

▲ **The Old King's Head Hotel 1921** 70562
This view looks through the entrance towards the inn yard, all of which survives to this day. Some of the ranges round the courtyard were galleried like those at the famous George Inn in Southwark, also owned by the National Trust. Owned by the Rothschilds from the 1870s, which probably preserved it from modernisation, the King's Head was given by them to the National Trust in 1926, five years after this photograph was taken.

◀ **The Bull's Head Hotel c1965** A84082
On the east side of Market Square was the Bull's Head Hotel, a mostly late 18th-century building which was Tudorised by Giacomo Gargini in the 1920s. A flamboyant character, and Mayor of Aylesbury in the 1930s, Gargini added the half-timbering, leaded windows and oriels, presumably to rival the genuine medieval framing of the King's Head. Demolished in 1969, it is now the entry to the early 1980s Hale Leys shopping centre.

Ye Olde Dark Lantern c1955 A84025
This now lost view looks from Market Street towards Silver Street: the timber-framed building on the left has been replaced by a 1970s building. To the right now is the east side of the vast Friars Square shopping centre. This is a brash and cheerily post-modern early 1990s reworking of a crudely brutalist 1960s concrete shopping precinct that had swept away much of the west side of the Market Square. The Dark Lantern beyond survives, and is a reminder of the maze of alleys in this area of market encroachment.

Walton Street 1921 70558

We are looking from Market Square south-east into Walton Street. The Bell had been reworked in 1919, and is still much the same. On the right, however, all has gone under the 1960s blizzard of redevelopment: the jewellers and the Greyhound Hotel made way for Friars Square shopping centre. Beyond is now 'Fred's Folly', the 1960s County Council office tower block, a landmark for miles around. It is of textured concrete and twelve storeys high, much disliked locally, but in fact a rather good design by Fred Pooley, the then County Architect.

Kingsbury Square 1901 47464

Kingsbury Square is the market place for the oldest part of the town; this grew up around the church, whose tower can be seen beyond the roofs. The square is actually triangular, with encroachment on the east side, and still recognisable a century after this view was taken. Until it was paved, it was often knee-deep in mud. The domestic elements have long gone - shops and pubs now occupy all the ground floors. The gardens and the houses on the left have been replaced by a routine 1960s block, Kingsbury House.

Left: **Victoria Hall 1897** 39627
The Victoria Club for Working Men in the west corner of Kingsbury is another benefaction from the Rothschilds, in this case Baron Ferdinand of Waddesdon. A stone plaque over the entrance records this as a commemoration of Queen Victoria's Jubilee, 21 June 1887. The building is still here, now the Victoria Club, with its sashes replaced by UPVC and the parapets rebuilt in simpler style.

Below: **The Children 1897** 39627x (extract from 39627)
Above the doorway can be seen the dedication plaque mentioned in the caption to photograph No 39627. The children, all in smart hats or bonnets, have mostly managed to stand still long enough for the photograph, except for the baby in the splendid period perambulator, whose head is a blur of activity. Are the children waiting patiently while their fathers take a glass or two of beer inside?

Left: **Kingsbury Square 1921** 70556
By this time, one of the houses has become a shop. The Red Lion on the left is now the Hobgoblin. In the centre of Kingsbury is the drinking fountain installed in 1914; it was removed in 1929 when a bus station was erected in the Square, and later re-erected in the Vale Park (see Chapter 2). Beyond is a World War I tank: it was parked here in 1920, but when it was being dismantled in 1929, it exploded - so it must have still contained some live ammunition for all those years.

Below: **Kingsbury c1955** A84112
This view shows the bus station that disfigured the open space of Kingsbury until the new bus station was built as part of the Friars Square development in the 1960s. The Red Lion has lost two of its ground floor sashes (they have since been reinstated), and Kingsbury House beyond replaced the shops. The Rookwood was much altered in the early 1950s, losing its sash windows and having its timber-framing covered over, and is now renamed the Lobster Pot.

Aylesbury:
The Town and the Outskirts

Left: **Temple Square c1955** A84024
The second chapter follows a series of routes radiating out from the Market Square and starts along Temple Street to Temple Square. This was probably a principal cross roads in the 10th-century Anglo-Saxon burh, with Kingsbury the market place at the south-east corner of the early town. Here the photographer looks from Temple Square along Church Street; the churchyard was also within the burh's earthen rampart.

Below: **Church Street c1955** A84100
In front of the Church is the County Museum; nearer the camera, behind the 'No Waiting' sign, is one of Aylesbury's best town houses, with arched sash windows to the ground floor. The brick front dates from 1739, and is a refronting of a mid 16th-century timber-framed house by Thomas Hickman, a native of Aylesbury born in 1695. He founded the Thomas Hickman charity, which built almshouses; it is an active housing charity still, buying and refurbishing houses and cottages in the old town for rent.

◄ **St Mary's Church c1955**
A84023
On the left are Hickman
Charity houses; the jettied
timber-framed cottages were
bought and refurbished in the
1980s, and the timber-
framing exposed. On the right
is the old Grammar School. It
was built from a bequest of
1714 and completed in 1720;
the rainwater heads are dated
1719. The stone doorcase
with its broken pediment was
carved in 1718. As it is now
the museum, the interiors can
be inspected and admired. In
the grounds is the modern
and immensely popular Roald
Dahl Gallery

◄ Church Street 1921 70559

All the houses on the left have been bought by the Thomas Hickman Charity in recent years and refurbished, including the Chantry on the left, a pretty Gothick front of about 1840 with arched and hood-moulded windows concealing a 16th century timber frame. On the right is the Buckinghamshire County Museum housed in Ceely House, the house with the porch on the right, and in the old Grammar School beyond. Ceely House's excellent Georgian front conceals a superb timber frame of 1472 built as the Brotherhood House of the Fraternity of the Virgin Mary.

▲ The Church 1927 79560

The main entrance to the churchyard where Church Street turns left to become Parsons Fee is distinguished by a pair of elegant early 18th-century gate piers in fine-jointed red brick surmounted by stone urn finials. Between are the remains of 18th century wrought iron gates and overthrow. The gateway seems to dwarf the children by the wall. The War Memorial to the left is in the form of a medieval calvary.

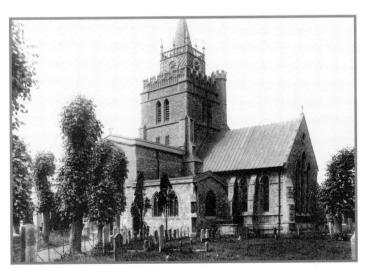

◄ The Parish Church 1897 39634

The large parish church is mostly 13th-century, but it was heavily restored by the great architect Sir George Gilbert Scott, a native of Buckinghamshire, between 1849 and 1869. It had got into a deplorable condition, and suffered a further mishap when the tower's parapets had to be removed some forty years ago. Its churchyard, though, is a haven of tranquillity in the centre of this busy town. There had been an Anglo-Saxon minster church here, and some of its foundations were found in excavations in 1978.

The Parish Church, The Chancel 1897 39636
This interior view of St Mary's Church looks east into the chancel past the central crossing under the tower. The Early English 13th-century Gothic-style lancets were inserted by Scott, who removed a large 15th-century east window. The interior has again been drastically re-ordered, including the construction of a stage at the west end from which the fine Norman font emerges incongruously. The 1978 repairs, though, stripped the grey cement wash off the columns and walls, so the interior is now a little brighter.

St Mary's Square c1955 A84022
We have turned right from Church Street. St Mary's Square is here no wider than a footpath, with the churchyard on the left. On the right is the 1840s brick Tudor-style old school, extended in replica in 1907. Beyond are cottages which were at one time the parish poorhouse, where the worthy poor made lace and baked bread. Behind the tree is the Bucks Evangelistic Mission, built in 1878 and replaced by the truly awful 1960s Granville Street Evangelical Church.

St Mary's Square c1965 A84116

Round the corner, the photographer looks back past the Bucks Evangelistic Mission hall to the Georgian-fronted cottages on the right of photograph No A84022. The windows on these houses are a mix of vertical sliding sashes, casements and horizontal sliding sashes, known as Norfolk sashes. Both trees in the churchyard survive today. On the far right is the old school on the corner of Pebble Lane, which leads back into Kingsbury; it is now an exhibition gallery for the County Museum.

Parsons Fee c1965 A84097

Parsons Fee leads south-west from Market Square past Prebendal House, the home of John Wilkes, the Radical MP for Aylesbury from 1757 to 1764, and behind high brick walls. The lane descends to Castle Street, from where this view was taken; we see St Osyths, a good brick house of 1700 with earlier timber-framed ranges, and the farmhouse to the Prebendal. Indeed, the great 16th-century tithe barn survives nearby.

▼ **Castle Street c1955** A84037

There was a castle at Aylesbury, but its location is unknown: only the name of Castle Street commemorates it. Here the photographer looks uphill towards Temple Square. The 18th-century cottages on the left stand behind a raised pavement. On the right is the tall pedimented front of the old Independent Chapel of 1778, demolished in 1979 and replaced by Hickman Charity flats.

▼ **County Offices c1965** A84062

The tour returns to Market Square and heads out along Walton Street at its south-east corner, past the County Offices of 1928 built in Neo-Georgian style in brick with stone dressings. These now face Fred's Folly, the concrete 1960s tower block. The hipped-roofed two storey house beyond survives, but not those beyond, which went for the Friarage Road/Exchange Street dual carriageway.

▲ **Walton Street 1901**

47465

Further south-east, the old village of Walton suffered greatly in the 1960s. The buildings on the left went to accommodate a dual-carriageway road widening. The church is Holy Trinity by David Brandon, built in the 1840s in flint pebbles and stone, with further Victorian additions in brick and stone. The rather good Georgian houses beyond went in 1927, to be replaced by Holy Trinity's Walton Parish Hall.

◀ Walton Pond c1955

A84002

A little further on we turn left into Walton Road; here, on the east side, is the village pond. Older houses nearby were destroyed or damaged by a World War II landmine, Aylesbury's only wartime bomb, which fell close to the pond. Opposite is a good Georgian brick house with smaller cottages to its left.

Cambridge Street
c1955 A84041
Back in the centre we head north-east out of Market Square along Cambridge Street, once known as Bakers Lane, a road that has seen much change since the 1950s. The Barley Corn pub survives, albeit now archly renamed the Farmyard and Firkin; the shop with the crested fascia, a pork butchers in the 1970s, is now The Bacon Shop, but the Old Harrow Inn has gone.

◀ **High Street 1897** 39625
The last radial tour from Market Square heads east and then east-south-east down the High Street, a street of houses until the later 19th century. This view captures some of the domestic feel of the lower High Street beyond the shops nearer Market Square. The facade on the left with the fully glazed first floor is Longley's, a drapery store, which was replaced by the present Marks and Spencer's building in 1938. Most of the buildings on the right some way downhill have now been rebuilt.

◀ **Cambridge Street c1955** A84028
Ye Olde Harrow Inn and the two-storey shops beyond went in the 1980s, but the tall three-storey brick building beyond of 1897 survives. Much beyond has also been replaced with 1980s work, while the old Odeon cinema, the blank wall in the distance, built in 1937, awaits demolition in 2000 for a Sainsbury's extension. More survives on the right as far as the middle distance, where the rear yard of Marks and Spencer's has punched a substantial hole in the street frontage.

▼ **The Wesleyan Chapel 1897** 39641
North-west from Kingsbury we go down Buckingham Street, passing the Wesleyan Church, now Aylesbury Methodist Church. The designers certainly pushed the boat out: their 1893 facade is stylishly Italianate, with lots of carved stonework, banded arches and granite columns. The gate piers and ironwork have gone, and the arches are now glazed in. The setting is not as good as it was in the 1890s, for the houses to the right, out of view, were replaced by awful 1960s shops with offices over.

◀ **The Bucks County Infirmary 1897** 39629
At the junction of Buckingham and Bicester Roads is the Royal Bucks Hospital. David Brandon rebuilt the hospital in 1859 to 1862 in a similar style to the earlier one; it had been a Georgian country house, with wings added in 1832. He was advised by Florence Nightingale herself, and it was the first post-Crimean War hospital to put into practice the Lady with the Lamp's precepts. It is remarkable that the facade is little changed, apart from an added storey at the right and a mansard to the centre.

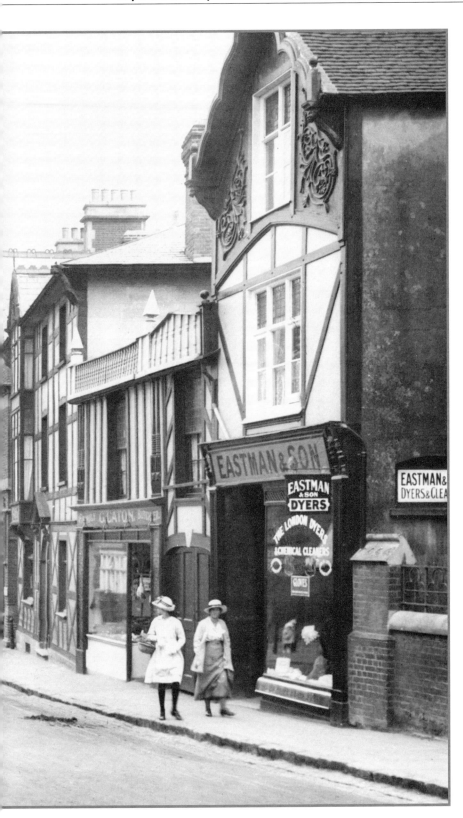

High Street 1921

70557
At the far right are the wall and railings belonging to the Congregational Church of 1874; its tower was kept when the church was demolished to make way for the Hale Leys Shopping Centre in 1988. Beyond is now MacDonalds and a modern post office. Further downhill, the houses now have single-storey shopfront projections. Further down, St Joseph's Catholic Church arrived in 1935: not a masterpiece, it has to be admitted, and in a pallid Gothic style.

High Street c1955 A84040
Looking back uphill towards Market Square, we move forward into the 1950s. The three-gabled 1850s stucco buildings on the left survive, but beyond all has been rebuilt up to the signpost. The bank on the right, 1920s extensions to two houses, went in 1975. Its drab replacement Nat West Bank is now Methvens booksellers. Beyond in the sunlight is the Market Square, with the unmistakable facade of Burtons visible.

High Street c1955 A84039
The photographer has turned east and is looking downhill in a similar location to the 1897 views. On the left is the 1938 neo-Georgian Marks and Spencer's that replaced Longleys. The rest of the buildings are in their last few years of existence. Of the 1850s terraces with white band course beyond Marks and Spencer's, only one house survives. In the far distance is the Hazell, Watson and Viney printing works with its tall chimney.

High Street c1955 A84057
The photographer has climbed onto the upper storey of the building next to Marks and Spencer's to look past the 1890s Post Office, the Tudor-style building with the ball finial to its gable on the right, to the Granada Cinema. The Post Office was demolished and replaced with the present characterless one in the 1960s, while the Granada has gone the way of so many cinemas and is now Gala Club Bingo.

High Street c1955 A84056
W H Smith's has moved uphill beyond Marks and Spencer's. Of this good 1830s terrace only two bays survive, those to the left of W H Smith, the pet and garden stores, which also retain the shopfront which was added to the house's facade. Marks and Spencer's share their 1938 neo-Georgian building with John Collier, 'the Window to Watch', as their slogan had it. Now defunct, it is a bathroom store.

◄ **The Vale c1950** A84007
Old Aylesbury was largely
confined to the hilltop
area; the surrounding land
was somewhat marshy
(and unhealthy). The High
Street was laid out in
1826 as New Road, but
development off the hill
was slow. The fields, now
The Vale Park, lay between
the railway station of 1839
and the gas works at the
foot of the hill and the
Bear Brook stream. By the
1880s part of it was the
town's cricket ground, so
it already had some public
use.

High Street c1955 A84055

The 'gateway' to the High Street at the Exchange Street junction has changed. The Chandos Arms and the shops beyond are now 1970s offices, and on the right side of the road is Hampden House, a stylish but incongruous office block with shops on the ground floor. St Joseph's Catholic Church is further up on the left, and Marks and Spencer's can be seen in the distance. Exchange Street was subsequently turned into a dual carriageway: the photographer stands where there is now a large roundabout.

The Vale c1955 A84053

The Park was formally opened on 1 July 1937. It is remarkably little changed, apart from the line of tall Lombardy poplars which went in the 1990s and the removal of the hedges. Even the flower beds are still planted and maintained. Beyond the trees on the right are football pitches and the former open-air swimming pool. The drinking fountain, the gift of Councillor Thomas Sheriff to the town in 1914, was moved here from Kingsbury (see photograph No 70556).

The Vale c1955 A84052

This view looks west towards one of two shelters, past the brick-walled sloping bed used for those 'say it with plants' commemorations so beloved of municipal gardeners everywhere. The shelter remains, but it has had the windows and brick infilling removed, so it now only shelters from the rain. Beyond the poplars was the old London and North West Railway station on the line from Cheddington. The station, by 1955 only for freight trains, was demolished in 1960.

The Milk Factory 1897 39640
This view is taken from the meadow beside the canal, the Aylesbury Arm of the Grand Union Canal, which opened in 1815. The meadow is now occupied by 1990s housing, Hilda Wharf. The factory is part of the Aylesbury Condensed Milk Company's works, which opened in 1870; it is now part of Nestle's. The left hand bay's top storey has gone and the ground floor windows are mostly blocked, but the building remains in use.

The Hazell, Watson and Viney Printing Works 1897 39638
Further out, where the High Street becomes Tring Road beyond the Walton Road and Park Street junction, the printing works of Hazell, Watson and Viney was built in 1878; its distinctive corner cupola and tall chimney are landmarks in the area. The junction was soon known as Hazell's Corner. In the foreground is the Burial Board's 1850s Aylesbury Cemetery, which survives, unlike the factory.

The Hazell, Watson and Viney Printing Works 1897 39639
This view looks east along Tring Road from Hazell's Corner. It is now a major roundabout, with a Tesco's on the left and the Works and house replaced. The house has gone for road 'improvement', and the printing works for the 1990s Wynn-Jones Centre, a collection of tyre-fitters and other industrial brick sheds. The municipal cemetery is in the distance, its railings and wall recently carefully repaired. Within are two Gothic-style stone chapels and a mortuary chapel, all of 1856.

The Aylesbury Arm Canal and Lock 1897 39643
This view looks south-west along the canal past the last lock, No 16, Hills and Partridges Lock, to Park Street Bridge. Hills and Partridges works have long gone; the site is now a Tesco's on the left out of view. The lock was the last before the narrow boats reached the canal basin at Walton Street, where a cargo crane is preserved. The bridge was rebuilt around 1900 by the Aylesbury Urban District Council in purple engineering brick. The building on the far left is the corner of the Nestle's works.

The Canal 1897 39642
The Aylesbury Arm was a branch from the Grand Junction Canal, later the Grand Union Canal, which ran from near Marsworth across the Vale to Aylesbury; it opened in 1815, twenty years after it was first authorised. This view looks along the towpath towards the Park Street bridge. The Nestle's factory is just out of sight on the right. The boys are fishing from a miniature wharf which still survives. On the left the meadow is now occupied by Hilda Wharf, 1990s housing.

Narbeth Drive c1965 A84068

After World War I, Aylesbury began developing along the arterial routes into the town. Along the Tring Road, the late 19th century saw the arrival of the factories and the cemetery seen in earlier views, and also housing developments such as the Edwardian Queen's Park or the 1890s Victoria Park. This took development as far east as the old main road which had turned south to Walton, now marked by King Edward's Avenue. From the 1920s, speculative semi-detached and detached villas sprang up further east: this is a typical 1960s example.

Tring Road c1965 A84065

This view looking towards town captures well the flavour of interwar development along the Tring Road itself. We can see tall lampposts, telephone line posts (still here), a bus stop and local shopping. The shop, the Tring Road Post Office (also punningly named 'The Andy Stores') at the junction of Limes Avenue, is just past the bay-windowed pair of semis on the left. The shop beyond it is now a dental clinic. Opposite, behind the bus stop, is a local doctor's surgery.

Westmorland Avenue c1965 A84079
Westmorland Avenue is one of the roads laid out for residential development between Tring Road and Wendover Road. These early 1950s houses are still pairs of semis with a mix of hipped and gabled roofs, the latter with rendered upper floors; they also have the metal-framed 'Crittal' windows which only went out of favour in the 1960s. Our tour of Aylesbury peters out amid the postwar expansion to accommodate London overspill.

A Tour East: from Aylesbury to Tring in Hertfordshire

Left: **Whiteleaf Cross and the Chilterns 1897**
39644
This photograph was taken from near Princes Risborough. The bare chalk in this view of the Whiteleaf Cross is nowadays not seen so clearly; the downs have since become covered in trees and scrub, with woods in the middle distant field. The Cross's origins are obscure. It is first mentioned in 1742, and theories vary from that it is a 9th-century Anglo-Danish battle commemoration to a form of outdoor poor relief in the 17th century.

Below: **Stoke Mandeville, The Hospital Driveway c1965** S569044
Now a centre of excellence in spinal injuries, Stoke Mandeville started as an isolation hospital, built in the 1930s. In this view the original hospital buildings show the stripped-down classicism used for the 1930s main block. The hospital has greatly expanded since, but the lime trees and the long drive to the main entrance remain.

◀ **Wendover, General View 1901** 44772
This long view of Wendover is taken from the opposite direction to No 44773, looking northeast from the foot of Bacombe Hill; here the national long distance footpath, the Ridgeway Path, leaves the road to climb towards Coombe Hill. In the middle distance is the railway line to Aylesbury, then part of the Metropolitan Railway and opened in 1891. There is now a by-pass, opened in 1997, in front of the railway.

Wendover, General View 1901 44773

The photographer is looking south-west across the pretty market town of Wendover, which lies on the edge of the Chilterns. The foreground field is now housing, Honey Banks and Hampden Road, with Bank Farm in the dip below. Beyond is the clocktower at the centre of the town. In the distance is Coombe Hill; since 1904, three years after this view, it has been dominated by a Boer War memorial obelisk.

Wendover, Aylesbury Street c1955 W51011

Aylesbury Road has probably the best run of historic buildings in any of Wendover's streets. Some good Georgian fronts hide timber-framed earlier buildings. Sturrick House, on the left, is an example, with its 18th-century rendered front concealing a 16th-century building, as does the stucco of the gabled house on the far right, Manor Farm House.

Wendover, Aylesbury Road c1965 W51033

We have moved nearer the High Street junction. The Red House on the left, one of the best houses in Wendover, is built in brick with earlier Georgian box sash windows with characteristic thick glazing bars and fine pedimented doorcases. On the right, The Old Cottage has its 17th-century timber-framing and jettied upper storey still exposed. Beyond is the clock tower.

Wendover, High Street 1901 47472
This view looks down the High Street towards the clock tower. This was built as a market hall and lock-up or temporary prison in 1842, but in 1870 the clocktower, belfry and spire were added. It is now a tourist information centre. The Two Brewers on the left is now an Italian restaurant, but the White Swan beyond is still a pub. The wall and trees on the right went for an access road to a public car park and library in the 1960s.

Wendover, Pound Street 1901 47471
Pound Street continues south-west from High Street; it is more cottagey, apart from two grander houses on the left. The street is little altered, apart from more formal pavements and roadway. The Georgian Shoulder of Mutton added this splendid plasterwork to its gable, and gave itself an alternative name to attract railway trade from the 1891 line to Aylesbury. Now it is again the Shoulder of Mutton only, and the rendered panel has been roughcast over.

Wendover, Coldharbour Cottages, Tring Road 1899 44771
At the opposite end of the High Street, the Tring Road climbs out of Wendover past this delightful range of early 17th-century timber-framed and thatched cottages. The brick and flint walls on the left were demolished for road widening; this took the 1960s concrete panel retaining wall near to Bank Farm, whose chimney is on the far left. The house incorporates a 15th-century hall house.

Tring, Tring Park 1897 39649
Our brief tour now crosses into Hertfordshire to Tring, a market town at the base of a salient of the county that projects into Buckinghamshire from the Chilterns along the valley of the River Bulbourne. Immediately south-east of the town is Tring Park, its park now bisected by the A41. The mansion incorporates a house designed by Sir Christopher Wren in the 1680s; it was enlarged and given a French Second Empire feel for Nathan Mayer Rothschild in the 1870s. It is now the Arts Educational School.

Tring, Tring Museum, The Zebra Room c1955 T81024
In buildings immediately west of Tring Park is housed the Sir Walter Rothschild Zoological Museum, based on his enormous collection of stuffed and mounted animals from every corner of the world. This view in the Zebra Room gives a good idea of the style of the museum; it is not to everyone's taste nowadays, although doubtless a tribute to the art of taxidermy.

Tring, High Street 1897 T81001
The town is a little disappointing - it is a mix of Rothschild fake timber-framing and earlier buildings. In this view the town is en fete for Queen Victoria's Diamond Jubilee. Much has gone, including the old Rose and Crown, which was replaced around 1900 by the present mock timber-framed one set back from the road: a townscape disaster. The building on the right with the navy flag has also gone to make a square in front of the church and war memorial.

◄ **New Mill, The Canal c1955** N153002
The new mill was built around 1800 to take advantage of the Grand Union Canal's Wendover Arm or branch canal that opened in 1797. The mill could take advantage of the canal for carrying its grain and flour all over the country. The Tringford Road bridge and the mill warehouse to the far right survive, but the canalside store with its bag hoist has been replaced by Heygate Flour, who now move everything by lorry.

Tring, High Street c1950

T81013

A little further west, the Bell on the right is a timber-framed coaching inn behind its late 18th-century painted brick facade. The dark archway on the left led into the Tring Brewery. In the distance is a group of 1890s brick buildings in the Dutch style fashionable at the time. Since the by-pass opened, the town has less traffic and the High Street has been paved with herring-bone paviours.

New Mill, The Village c1955 N153005

The hamlet of New Mill grew up near the canal north of Tring around Tring Mill, now Heygate Flour. The mill was built as a corn mill, and mill workers' cottages grew up along the Tringford Road, complete with an 1870s elementary school. This view looks south-west along the Bulbourne Road, with 1890s cottages on the left and the New Mill Social Centre on the right.

New Mill, The Village c1955 N153006

We are at the junction of Wingrave Road on the left, which leads into Tring past the site of the old Tring silk mill, and Tringford Road on the right; the photographer is standing in Bulbourne Road where it meets the Icknield Way, which goes straight on past the 1950s council houses. The Queen's Arms pub of about 1840 provided a social centre for New Mill, but it was demolished for road improvement some twenty years ago.

Left: Tring, Marsworth Locks c1960 T81054
Half a mile north of New Mill is a complex of
reservoirs; they were built by the Grand Junction Canal
in the 1830s to store water for the Marsworth Flight of
locks, whereby the canal descends from the Tring Gap
onto the Vale of Aylesbury. These are now nature
reserves and popular with walkers, as is the canal
towpath itself. Here at Lock 39 the Lower Icknield Way
crosses the canal beside the White Lion pub, which
was built to slake the thirst of bargees in the mid 19th
century.

Below: Tring, Pendley Manor c1955 T81023
The present Pendley Manor replaced a complex
medieval and later house which burnt down in 1835.
This architecturally busy Tudorbethan house, built after
1871, is now a hotel and conference centre set in
tranquil parkland; that parkland came into being
through the 1440s destruction of a large village by the
then owner, Sir Robert Wittingham, to make himself a
deer park.

A Tour West from Aylesbury

Hartwell, The Egyptian Springs 1901 47467
Our tour starts with a piece of exotica on the lane to
Lower Hartwell. Built in 1851 by the then owner of
Hartwell House, Dr John Lee, a noted amateur
Egyptologist and archaeologist, this building with
Egyptian hieroglyphs has now been beautifully
restored. The cornice has been remade and its Greek
inscription reinstated - it reads: 'Ariston men Hudor',
'water is best', a quotation from one of Pindar's
'Olympian Odes'. Hartwell House itself, a mainly
Jacobean mansion, is now a fine country house hotel.

Aylesbury, The County Asylum, Stone 1897 39630
The County Lunatic Asylum was built at Stone, three miles west of Aylesbury, in the early 1850s by the architects Thomas Wyatt and David Brandon. Later renamed St John's Hospital for more sensitive times, the whole building was demolished in the late 1990s. A shame, as the restrained (or should I say economical?) Italianate style of the buildings and their elegant sash windows would have converted well to apartments.

Aylesbury, The County Asylum, Stone 1897 39632
This view looks towards the main entrance ranges, which were altered and added to by Brandon in the 1860s and 1870s. On the left, out of view, is Brandon's chapel, a surprisingly large cruciform Gothic-style stone church of the 1860s and the only building to survive the housing estate deluge that replaced the hospital. Unfortunately, as I write it has not yet found a new use. To fix your bearings, the drive in this view is now Warren Close, one of the 1990s housing estate roads.

Haddenham, Banks Pond c1960 H375036
Haddenham was one of the chief breeding areas for the Aylesbury duck; its network of streams and ponds was of immense value to this industry, even if the village was famously foul-smelling in a hot summer. This is one of the ponds, Banks Pond, on the main east-west road through the village; the scene is relatively unchanged, although out of view to the left is now a parade of 1960s shops.

Haddenham, Church End Green c1955 H375006
Down at Church End there is another more well-known and photographed pond; it and the 13th-century parish church are to the left of the War Memorial. This view shows the characteristic rendered walls of the village houses. The render hides walls built in the local limey clay known as 'witchert', a corruption of white earth. Alcohol is also well represented here: the house on the right was the maltster's, the maltings being in the yard behind, while two other houses in this view were once pubs.

Upper Winchendon, The Wilderness 1897

39666
Climbing out of the Vale of Aylesbury northwards onto the Brill-Winchendon Hills, we reach Upper Winchendon, where the Marquess of Wharton built a vast country house around 1700. Demolished in 1758, only the service range survives; it was converted into a house, which is now occupied by the estate manager of the Rothschild lands around Waddesdon, Winchendon and Tythrop. Behind is the Norman church where John Wesley preached his first sermon after his ordination.

▼ Waddesdon Manor, North Front 1897 39657

At the summit of Lodge Hill to the north of the Upper Winchendon ridge is a French chateau. It was built by a French architect with the splendidly florid name Hippolyte Alexandre Gabriel Walter Destailleur for Baron Ferdinand de Rothschild, who had bought the estate in 1872. Lodge Hill was then a bare hill, but the Baron imported vast numbers of mature trees to give it its present wooded character; teams of horses toiled from far and wide to haul the trees to their destination.

▼ Waddesdon Manor, South Front 1897 39653

The hill top was levelled to accommodate the house, its parterres and approaches, and a fine aviary was added in 1889. The design draws on a number of French chateaux; it has a wonderfully complex roofscape, while inside is a spectacular collection of panelling, chimneypieces, boiseries and fittings salvaged from French mansions, as well as priceless collections of porcelain and other antiques. It is now an immensely popular attraction owned by the National Trust.

▲ Waddesdon, The Five Arrows Hotel 1901

47469

Ferdinand de Rothschild also reworked the village, this time choosing a picturesque Olde English style with lots of half-timbering and ornate chimney stacks. His architect was Taylor, from Bierton, a village near Aylesbury; he was heavily influenced by George Devey, who had worked for Meyer de Rothschild at Ascott House, near Wing. The Five Arrows Hotel is the best of these Rothschild buildings, dated 1887.

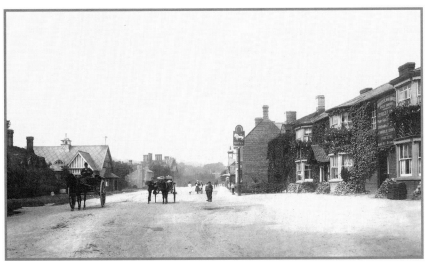

◀ **Waddesdon, The Village and the White Lion Hotel 1901** 47470

In the distance is the Five Arrows Hotel; the five arrows symbolise the five Rothschild brothers - the badge is seen on houses and cottages all over central Buckinghamshire. On the left are the Goodwin Almshouses, founded in 1642 but rebuilt by Ferdinand de Rothschild in 1893, and beyond is the full-blown Arts and Crafts style Waddesdon village hall of 1897, also built by Rothschild. The Lion pub on the right pre-dates the Rothschild era.

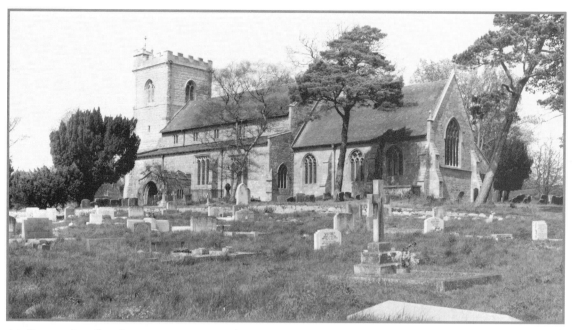

Quainton, The Church c1955 Q14024
Quainton is nowadays noted for its steam railway collection and tower windmill. Its church houses a superb collection of monuments to the 17th- and 18th-century Dormer family. The medieval church itself was substantially rebuilt in the 1870s reusing much of the stone and windows. This view from the south-east corner of the churchyard is little changed, although the yew is bigger. The pine by the chancel survives, but there is now a vulgar yellow conifer disrupting the view.

Oving, The Village c1955 O118006
Moving north-east of Waddesdon, the last two villages on this tour, Oving and Whitchurch, are on the Quainton-Whitchurch Hills, a ridge of Portland limestone that gives fine views over the Vale of Aylesbury to the south and towards Buckingham to the north. Oving is a most attractive village. Here we see Magpie Cottage, a fine 17th-century timber-framed thatched cottage with whitewashed infill panels, hence the name, presumably.

Oving, The Black Boy Inn c1955 0118004
From the rear of the Black Boy are fine views towards North Marston, the hill dropping sharply into the valley. The famous inn is a mix of various periods, including a 17th-century timber-framed core. In these racially more sensitive days, the sign now shows what appears to be a collier's boy, his face covered in coal dust, rather than the caricature seen in this view!

Oving, The Church and the Black Boy Inn c1955 0118002
The Black Boy is on the left, with the Victorian school, now a house, beyond the car. The ugly lean-to on the cottage has been replaced by a conservatory, and the railings by a rubble stone wall. The church, like Quainton's, was substantially rebuilt, this time in the 1860s, a not uncommon result of medieval use of the local highly friable limestone.

Oving, The Post Office c1955 O118009
This view is taken looking south towards Oving from Bowling Alley's junction with the North Marston to Whitchurch Road.
The carrier's wagon outside the post office gives an old-fashioned feel to this 1950s view - but milk floats and rag and
bone carts were also still horse-drawn well into the late 1950s. The outbuilding and shop beyond have been demolished;
the site is occupied by new houses. The slate-roofed house by the telegraph pole survives, but nothing else is the same
on the left side of the road.

Whitchurch, Oving Road c1955 W433002
Moving east, the route passes through Whitchurch on its way back to Aylesbury. Whitchurch is a long village with many
fine houses and cottages, and also the remains of Hugh of Bolbec's early 12th-century earthwork castle. Oving Road runs
east from the High Street; this view is taken beyond its junction with Market Hill looking west, showing the mix of building
materials found in the village: timber-framing, brick, local crumbly limestone, thatch, tiles and slate.

Whitchurch, Market Hill c1955 W433001
The lord of the manor, Hugh de Vere, Earl of Oxford, was granted a market charter in 1245. He laid out a market place outside the castle ramparts which still survives, although it is somewhat encroached upon. It was never a very successful one, and was unable to compete with Aylesbury, Winslow and Buckingham markets. By the end of the Middle Ages it had ceased to function, and the town reverted to a large village.

Whitchurch, High Street c1955 W433006
The High Street is a long one on the main Aylesbury to Buckingham road. This view, looking south towards Aylesbury, shows some of the range of buildings, including the rendered and jettied Tudor House in the middle distance. The church is off a lane to the left out of the picture. The road is needless to say considerably more busy nowadays, and we head down it back to Aylesbury and the end of this chapter's western tour.

Index

Frith Book Co Titles

www.frithbook.co.uk

The Frith Book Company publishes over 100 new titles each year. A selection of those currently available are listed below. For latest catalogue please contact Frith Book Co.

Town Books 96pp, 100 photos. County and Themed Books 128pp, 150 photos (unless specified). All titles hardback laminated case and jacket except those indicated pb (paperback)

Around Bakewell	1-85937-113-2	£12.99	Around Great Yarmouth	1-85937-085-3	£12.99
Around Barnstaple	1-85937-084-5	£12.99	Around Guildford	1-85937-117-5	£12.99
Around Bath	1-85937-097-7	£12.99	Hampshire	1-85937-064-0	£14.99
Berkshire (pb)	1-85937-191-4	£9.99	Around Harrogate	1-85937-112-4	£12.99
Around Blackpool	1-85937-049-7	£12.99	Around Horsham	1-85937-127-2	£12.99
Around Bognor Regis	1-85937-055-1	£12.99	Around Ipswich	1-85937-133-7	£12.99
Around Bournemouth	1-85937-067-5	£12.99	Ireland (pb)	1-85937-181-7	£9.99
Brighton (pb)	1-85937-192-2	£8.99	Isle of Man	1-85937-065-9	£14.99
British Life A Century Ago	1-85937-103-5	£17.99	Isle of Wight	1-85937-114-0	£14.99
Buckinghamshire (pb)	1-85937-200-7	£9.99	Kent (pb)	1-85937-189-2	£9.99
Around Cambridge	1-85937-092-6	£12.99	Around Leicester	1-85937-073-x	£12.99
Cambridgeshire	1-85937-086-1	£14.99	Leicestershire (pb)	1-85937-185-x	£9.99
Canals and Waterways	1-85937-129-9	£17.99	Around Lincoln	1-85937-111-6	£12.99
Cheshire	1-85937-045-4	£14.99	Lincolnshire	1-85937-135-3	£14.99
Around Chester	1-85937-090-x	£12.99	London (pb)	1-85937-183-3	£9.99
Around Chichester	1-85937-089-6	£12.99	Around Maidstone	1-85937-056-x	£12.99
Churches of Berkshire	1-85937-170-1	£17.99	New Forest	1-85937-128-0	£14.99
Churches of Dorset	1-85937-172-8	£17.99	Around Newark	1-85937-105-1	£12.99
Colchester (pb)	1-85937-188-4	£8.99	Around Newquay	1-85937-140-x	£12.99
Cornwall	1-85937-054-3	£14.99	North Devon Coast	1-85937-146-9	£14.99
Cumbria	1-85937-101-9	£14.99	Northumberland and Tyne & Wear		
Dartmoor	1-85937-145-0	£14.99		1-85937-072-1	£14.99
Around Derby	1-85937-046-2	£12.99	Norwich (pb)	1-85937-194-9	£8.99
Derbyshire (pb)	1-85937-196-5	£9.99	Around Nottingham	1-85937-060-8	£12.99
Devon	1-85937-052-7	£14.99	Nottinghamshire (pb)	1-85937-187-6	£9.99
Dorset	1-85937-075-6	£14.99	Around Oxford	1-85937-096-9	£12.99
Dorset Coast	1-85937-062-4	£14.99	Oxfordshire	1-85937-076-4	£14.99
Down the Severn	1-85937-118-3	£14.99	Peak District	1-85937-100-0	£14.99
Down the Thames	1-85937-121-3	£14.99	Around Penzance	1-85937-069-1	£12.99
Around Dublin	1-85937-058-6	£12.99	Around Plymouth	1-85937-119-1	£12.99
East Sussex	1-85937-130-2	£14.99	Around St Ives	1-85937-068-3	£12.99
Around Eastbourne	1-85937-061-6	£12.99	Around Scarborough	1-85937-104-3	£12.99
Edinburgh (pb)	1-85937-193-0	£8.99	Scotland (pb)	1-85937-182-5	£9.99
English Castles	1-85937-078-0	£14.99	Scottish Castles	1-85937-077-2	£14.99
Essex	1-85937-082-9	£14.99	Around Sevenoaks and Tonbridge		
Around Exeter	1-85937-126-4	£12.99		1-85937-057-8	£12.99
Exmoor	1-85937-132-9	£14.99	Around Southampton	1-85937-088-8	£12.99
Around Falmouth	1-85937-066-7	£12.99	Around Southport	1-85937-106-x	£12.99

Available from your local bookshop or from the publisher

Frith Book Co Titles (continued)

Scottish Castles	1-85937-077-2	£14.99		Around Torbay	1-85937-063-2	£12.99
Around Sevenoaks and Tonbridge	1-85937-057-8	£12.99		Around Truro	1-85937-147-7	£12.99
Around Southampton	1-85937-088-8	£12.99		Victorian & Edwardian Kent	1-85937-149-3	£14.99
Around Southport	1-85937-106-x	£12.99		Victorian & Edwardian Maritime Album		
Around Shrewsbury	1-85937-110-8	£12.99			1-85937-144-2	£17.99
Shropshire	1-85937-083-7	£14.99		Victorian & Edwardian Yorkshire	1-85937-154-x	£14.99
South Devon Coast	1-85937-107-8	£14.99		Victorian Seaside	1-85937-159-0	£17.99
South Devon Living Memories	1-85937-168-x	£14.99		Warwickshire (pb)	1-85937-203-1	£9.99
Staffordshire (96pp)	1-85937-047-0	£12.99		Welsh Castles	1-85937-120-5	£14.99
Stone Circles & Ancient Monuments				West Midlands	1-85937-109-4	£14.99
	1-85937-143-4	£17.99		West Sussex	1-85937-148-5	£14.99
Around Stratford upon Avon	1-85937-098-5	£12.99		Wiltshire	1-85937-053-5	£14.99
Sussex (pb)	1-85937-184-1	£9.99		Around Winchester	1-85937-139-6	£12.99

Frith Book Co titles available Autumn 2000

Cotswolds (pb)	1-85937-230-9	£9.99	Sep	English Country Houses	1-85937-161-2	£17.99	Oct
Cornish Coast	1-85937-163-9	£14.99	Sep	Folkestone (pb)	1-85937-124-8	£9.99	Oct
County Durham	1-85937-123-x	£14.99	Sep	Humberside	1-85937-215-5	£14.99	Oct
Dorset Living Memories	1-85937-210-4	£14.99	Sep	Manchester (pb)	1-85937-198-1	£9.99	Oct
Dublin (pb)	1-85937-231-7	£9.99	Sep	Norfolk Living Memories	1-85937-217-1	£14.99	Oct
Herefordshire	1-85937-174-4	£14.99	Sep	Preston (pb)	1-85937-212-0	£9.99	Oct
Kent Living Memories	1-85937-125-6	£14.99	Sep	Reading (pb)	1-85937-238-4	£9.99	Oct
Leeds (pb)	1-85937-202-3	£9.99	Sep	Salisbury (pb)	1-85937-239-2	£9.99	Oct
Ludlow (pb)	1-85937-176-0	£9.99	Sep	South Hams	1-85937-220-1	£14.99	Oct
Norfolk (pb)	1-85937-195-7	£9.99	Sep	Suffolk (pb)	1-85937-221-x	£9.99	Oct
North Yorks (pb)	1-85937-236-8	£9.99	Sep	Swansea (pb)	1-85937-167-1	£9.99	Oct
Somerset	1-85937-153-1	£14.99	Sep	West Yorkshire (pb)	1-85937-201-5	£9.99	Oct
Surrey (pb)	1-85937-240-6	£9.99	Sep				
Tees Valley & Cleveland	1-85937-211-2	£14.99	Sep	Around Aylesbury (pb)	1-85937-227-9	£9.99	Nov
Thanet (pb)	1-85937-116-7	£9.99	Sep	Around Bradford (pb)	1-85937-204-x	£9.99	Nov
Tiverton (pb)	1-85937-178-7	£9.99	Sep	Around Chichester (pb)	1-85937-228-7	£9.99	Nov
Victorian and Edwardian Sussex				East Anglia (pb)	1-85937-265-1	£9.99	Nov
	1-85937-157-4	£14.99	Sep	East London	1-85937-080-2	£14.99	Nov
Weymouth (pb)	1-85937-209-0	£9.99	Sep	Gloucestershire	1-85937-102-7	£14.99	Nov
Worcestershire	1-85937-152-3	£14.99	Sep	Greater Manchester (pb)	1-85937-266-x	£9.99	Nov
Yorkshire Living Memories	1-85937-166-3	£14.99	Sep	Hastings & Bexhill (pb)	1-85937-131-0	£9.99	Nov
				Helston (pb)	1-85937-214-7	£9.99	Nov
British Life A Century Ago (pb)				Lancaster, Morecombe & Heysham (pb)			
	1-85937-213-9	£9.99	Oct		1-85937-233-3	£9.99	Nov
Camberley (pb)	1-85937-222-8	£9.99	Oct	Peterborough (pb)	1-85937-219-8	£9.99	Nov
Cardiff (pb)	1-85937-093-4	£9.99	Oct	Piers	1-85937-237-6	£17.99	Nov
Carmarthenshire	1-85937-216-3	£14.99	Oct	Wiltshire Living Memories	1-85937-245-7	£14.99	Nov
Cheltenham (pb)	1-85937-095-0	£9.99	Oct	Windmills & Watermills	1-85937-242-2	£17.99	Nov
Cornwall (pb)	1-85937-229-5	£9.99	Oct	York (pb)	1-85937-199-x	£9.99	Nov

See Frith books on the internet www.frithbook.co.uk

FRITH PRODUCTS & SERVICES

Francis Frith would doubtless be pleased to know that the pioneering publishing venture he started in 1860 still continues today. A hundred and forty years later, The Francis Frith Collection continues in the same innovative tradition and is now one of the foremost publishers of vintage photographs in the world. Some of the current activities include:

Interior Decoration

Today Frith's photographs can be seen framed and as giant wall murals in thousands of pubs, restaurants, hotels, banks, retail stores and other public buildings throughout the country. In every case they enhance the unique local atmosphere of the places they depict and provide reminders of gentler days in an increasingly busy and frenetic world.

Product Promotions

Frith products are used by many major companies to promote the sales of their own products or to reinforce their own history and heritage. Frith promotions have been used by Hovis bread, Courage beers, Scots Porage Oats, Colman's mustard, Cadbury's foods, Mellow Birds coffee, Dunhill pipe tobacco, Guinness, and Bulmer's Cider.

Genealogy and Family History

As the interest in family history and roots grows world-wide, more and more people are turning to Frith's photographs of Great Britain for images of the towns, villages and streets where their ancestors lived; and, of course, photographs of the churches and chapels where their ancestors were christened, married and buried are an essential part of every genealogy tree and family album.

Frith Products

All Frith photographs are available Framed or just as Mounted Prints and Posters (size 23 x 16 inches). These may be ordered from the address below. From time to time other products - Address Books, Calendars, Table Mats, etc - are available.

The Internet

Already twenty thousand Frith photographs can be viewed and purchased on the internet. By the end of the year 2000 some 60,000 Frith photographs will be available on the internet. The number of sites is constantly expanding, each focussing on different products and services from the Collection.
The main Frith sites are listed below.
www.francisfrith.co.uk
www.frithbook.co.uk

See the complete list of Frith Books at:

www.frithbook.co.uk

This web site is regularly updated with the latest list of publications from the Frith Book Company. If you wish to buy books relating to another part of the country that your local bookshop does not stock, you may purchase on-line.

For further information, trade, or author enquiries please contact us at the address below:
The Francis Frith Collection, Frith's Barn, Teffont, Salisbury, Wiltshire, England SP3 5QP.
Tel: +44 (0)1722 716 376 Fax: +44 (0)1722 716 881 Email: uksales@francisfrith.com

See Frith books on the internet www.frithbook.co.uk

TO RECEIVE YOUR FREE MOUNTED PRINT

Mounted Print
Overall size 14 x 11 inches

Cut out this Voucher and return it with your remittance for £1.50 to cover postage and handling, to UK addresses. For overseas addresses please include £4.00 post and handling. Choose any photograph included in this book. Your SEPIA print will be A4 in size, and mounted in a cream mount with burgundy rule lines, overall size 14 x 11 inches.

Order additional Mounted Prints at HALF PRICE (only £7.49 each*)

If there are further pictures you would like to order, possibly as gifts for friends and family, purchase them at half price (no additional postage and handling required).

Have your Mounted Prints framed*

For an additional £14.95 per print you can have your chosen Mounted Print framed in an elegant polished wood and gilt moulding, overall size 16 x 13 inches (no additional postage and handling required).

---

* IMPORTANT!
These special prices are only available if ordered using the original voucher on this page (no copies permitted) and at the same time as your free Mounted Print, for delivery to the same address

---

Frith Collectors' Guild

From time to time we publish a magazine of news and stories about Frith photographs and further special offers of Frith products. If you would like 12 months FREE membership, please return this form.

Send completed forms to:
The Francis Frith Collection, Frith's Barn, Teffont, Salisbury, Wiltshire SP3 5QP

$\mathcal{V}$oucher for **FREE** and Reduced Price Frith Prints

Picture no.	Page number	Qty	Mounted @ £7.49	Framed + £14.95	Total Cost
		1	Free of charge*	£	£
			£7.49	£	£
			£7.49	£	£
			£7.49	£	£
			£7.49	£	£
			£7.49	£	£

Please allow 28 days for delivery	*** Post & handling**	**£1.50**
Book Title	**Total Order Cost**	**£**

Please do not photocopy this voucher. Only the original is valid, so please cut it out and return it to us.

I enclose a cheque / postal order for £ . . . .
made payable to 'The Francis Frith Collection'
OR please debit my Mastercard / Visa / Switch / Amex card
(credit cards please on all overseas orders)

Number . . . .

Issue No(Switch only) . . . . .Valid from (Amex/Switch) . . . .

Expires . . . . Signature . . . .

Name Mr/Mrs/Ms . . . .

Address . . . .

. . . .

. . . . Postcode . . . .

Daytime Tel No . . . .   Valid to 31/12/02

The Francis Frith Collectors' Guild

Please enrol me as a member for 12 months free of charge.

Name Mr/Mrs/Ms . . . .

Address . . . .

. . . .

. . . . Postcode . . . .

Free Print - see overleaf